'alks

Text: *Vivienne Crow*
Series editor: *Tony Bowerman*
Photographs: *Vivienne Crow, Steve Thompson/ www.sunstormphotography.com, Paul Merry, Carl Rogers, Shutterstock, Dreamstime*

Design: *Carl Rogers*

Northern Eye Books

ISBN 978-1-908632-21-0

A CIP catalogue record for this book is available from the British Library.

Important Advice: The routes described in this book are undertaken at the reader's own risk. Walkers should take into account their level of fitness, wear suitable footwear and clothing, and carry food and water. It is also advisable to take the relevant OS map with you in case you get lost and leave the area covered by our maps.

Whilst every care has been taken to ensure the accuracy of the route directions, the publishers cannot accept responsibility for errors or omissions, or for changes in the details given. Nor can the publisher and copyright owners accept responsibility for any consequences arising from the use of this book.

If you find any inaccuracies in either the text or maps, please write or email us at the address below. Thank you.

First published in 2013 by

Northern Eye Books Limited
Northern Eye Books, Tattenhall, Cheshire CH3 9PX
Email: tony@northerneyebooks.com

For sales enquiries, please call 01928 723 744

Cover: *Bluebells in Staveley woods (Walk 3)*
Photo: Shutterstock/Jay Warren

www.northerneyebooks.co.uk
www.top10walks.co.uk
www.walkuk.co.uk

 Twitter: @viviennecrow2
@Northerneyeboo
@Top10walks

Contents

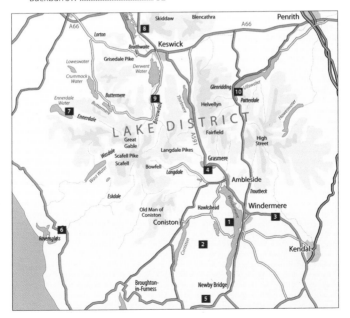

England's Largest National Park

THE LAKE DISTRICT NATIONAL PARK is the largest and most popular of the thirteen National Parks in England and Wales. Created as one of Britain's first National Parks in 1951, its role is to 'conserve and enhance' the natural beauty, wildlife and culture of this iconic English landscape, not just for residents and visitors today but for future generations, too.

Remarkably, the National Park contains every scrap of England's land over 3,000 feet, including its highest mountain, Scafell Pike. Packed within the Park's 885 square miles are numerous peaks and fells, over 400 lakes and tarns, around 50 dales, six National Nature Reserves, and more than 100 Sites of Special Scientific Interest—all publicly accessible on over 1,800 miles of footpaths and other rights of way. It's no surprise then, that the Lake District attracts an estimated 15 million visitors a year.

Fragrant bluebells carpet the floor of a Cumbrian wood in spring

Lake District woodland walks

Humans seem to be drawn to trees, be they part of a landscape that has existed for centuries or planted in more modern times. There is something special about being in among their sturdy trunks, surrounded by a rich understorey with the sunlight piercing the canopy high above. In the Lake District, there is a huge variety of woodland — and no matter what their origins, what tree types grow there or how they have been managed, that extraordinary atmosphere never fails to nourish the soul.

"Who hath not felt the influence that so calms
The weary mind in summer's sultry hours
When wandering thickest woods beneath the arms
Of ancient oaks and brushing nameless flowers."

John Clare, *Wood Rides*, c.1822

TOP 10 **Walks:** The Best Woodland Walks

WE ALL HAVE OUR IMAGES OF WHAT A 'WALK IN THE WOODS' should be like, but each woodland has its own character. And, as the seasons progress, even that unique personality changes. The ten walks featured here cover a vast range of woodland types: from the ancient oak and birch woods of Borrowdale to the plantations of Grizedale. Spring flowers, autumn colours, wildlife, riverside trails, mountain views, lakes and even a mysterious monk feature on these routes throughout the National Park.

Claife Heights — page 8

Grizedale Forest — page 14

Staveley's woods — page 20

Grasmere's woods — page 26

Wise Een Tarn and the Langdale Pikes

Claife Heights

An easy, low-level walk through rolling hills and atmospheric forest, ending with a lakeside stroll

Distance/time: 10km/ 6 miles. Allow 2½-3 hours

Start: Small car park (with honesty box) at Braithwaite Hall, diagonally opposite the Cuckoo Brow Inn in Far Sawrey

Grid ref: SD 379 954

Ordnance Survey Map: Explorer OL7 The English Lakes South-eastern area, *Windermere, Kendal & Silverdale*

After the walk: Cuckoo Brow Inn, Far Sawrey, Ambleside, Cumbria LA22 0LQ | www.cuckoobrow.co.uk | 01539 443425 | stay@cuckoobrow.co.uk

Walk outline

This gentle saunter to the west of Windermere starts by following a good track from Far Sawrey to two tarns — the pretty Moss Eccles and the gorgeously situated Wise Een. It then enters the supposedly haunted forests of Claife Heights before dropping to Windermere's wooded shores. A long lakeside walk is followed by roadside paths and lanes climbing gently back up to Far Sawrey.

Claife Heights

The western shores of Windermere are cloaked in luscious woodland — practically all the way from Wray Castle in the north to Lakeside in the south. The most substantial area of forest is the National Trust-owned Claife Heights. This consists mostly of mixed woodland with a few small conifer plantations scattered amongst them. Oak, alder, birch and larch are the most common tree species.

The gently rolling landscape is dotted with rocky knolls, mires and tarns, providing breaks in the tree cover and giving walkers an opportunity to enjoy lovely views of the nearby fells.

Moss Eccles Tarn

Red deer stag

The Walk

1. Turn left along the road, passing the **Cuckoo Brow Inn**, and then take the next road on the right (**Cuckoo Brow Lane**). About 130 metres after crossing a cattle grid, bear left along a track. You will later join another track coming up from the left as you continue uphill to **Moss Eccles Tarn**.

2. Beyond this pretty spot, the track continues climbing until you reach a gate. Going through, you are met by a wonderful vista: **Wise Een Tarn** is laid out before you and, behind it, seemingly just a stone's throw away, are the **Langdale Pikes**. As the track swings right, **Bow Fell** and **Crinkle Crags** also appear. The track briefly becomes a little less distinct as it climbs a grassy slope and then enters the forest via a gate.

It now seems appropriate — before heading any deeper into the dark forest — to warn readers about the Claife Crier... One stormy night, a long, long time ago, the ferrymen of Windermere heard an eerie voice summoning them from the western shores of the lake. Most chose to ignore the call, but one young oarsman set off to collect his fare. He returned several hours later, ashen-faced and struck dumb. What had happened to him out there on the lake? What had he seen? His colleagues never found out for he soon developed a fever and, within days, was dead.

The voice continued to call out from the Claife Heights on wild nights, but the ferrymen ignored it. Finally, a priest was called in to exorcise it — and the spirit was silenced.

First light: *Boathouse on Wise Een Tarn*

There have been several theories to explain the origins of the so-called Claife Crier. It has been suggested that it was 'an echo' of one of the tragedies that occurred on Windermere in the 17th century. In 1635 and again in 1681, two boats sank, drowning all onboard. In the first accident, 47 wedding guests were killed on their way home from the ceremony.

Another, more popular, theory is that the calls came from the ghost of a monk from Furness Abbey who was prevented from marrying the woman he loved by his monastic vows. Tormented, he retreated to the forests of Claife where he died of grief. Some people claim to have seen his hooded figure wandering the forest tracks after dark.

3. Assuming that story hasn't put you off, follow the clear track for about 350 metres and then turn left along a stony trail heading downhill. When this crosses another forest track, keep heading straight downhill. The felled areas here open up a new vista to walkers as the long, grassy ridges of the eastern fells

Out on the water: *Yachts moored against the backdrop of Windermere's wooded shore*

put in an appearance on the horizon. At the next forest road, cross straight over and head down the rough track opposite — towards **Belle Grange**.

4. Just after passing a large white house on your left, you reach a T-junction. Turn right along the wide track beside the lake.

5. Eventually, you reach a road junction. Turn right here and, almost immediately, go through a gap in the wall on the right. At the top of the initial climb, bear left, ascending more gently now with superb views down **Windermere**. Just before reaching the ruins of **Claife Station**, turn left down a set of stone steps. At the bottom, turn right, following signs for Hill Top. Cross the **National Trust car park** to pick up a path to the right of wall, parallel with the road. Once through the next gate, cross the road and pick up the continuation of the roadside path on the other side. After the next gate, continue along the **B5285** towards **Far Sawrey**.

6. When the road bends left, close to a bench, turn right along a rough, stony track. Cross straight over a surfaced track and go through a kissing-gate.

You soon reach another surfaced lane. Keep straight ahead, around the front of the buildings with a wall on your right. Go through a metal kissing-gate and then drop down the shady track.

You come out on the road opposite the **Braithwaite Hall car park** in **Far Sawrey**. ◆

Pottering about?

Moss Eccles Tarn was bought by the children's writer Beatrix Potter in 1913, the year she married William Heelis. The couple kept a boat on the tarn and spent many happy summer evenings here — he fishing, she sketching. They also planted one red water lily and one white water lily. It's now a Site of Special Scientific Interest with a range of aquatic plants as well as plentiful damselflies and dragonflies.

Looking down from the rocky summit of Carron Crag

Grizedale Forest

An excellent hike through a huge, sprawling forest with superb views from a rocky vantage point

What to expect:
Good forest trails and tracks; rough path on Carron Crag

Distance/time: 8km/ 5 miles. Allow 2½-3 hours

Start: Moor Top pay and display car park close to the northern edge of Grizedale Forest

Grid ref: SD 342 965

Ordnance Survey Maps: Explorer OL7 The English Lakes *South-eastern area, Windermere, Kendal & Silverdale*

After the walk: Café in the Forest, Grizedale Forest, Hawkshead, Ambleside, Cumbria LA22 0QJ | www.breweryarts.co.uk/food-and-drink/cafe-in-the-forest | 01229 860455 | info@breweryarts.co.uk

Walk outline

The first half of this walk is on good tracks and paths through the vast conifer plantations that cover Grizedale Moor. Poking its rocky head above this blanket of trees is Carron Crag: at 314 metres, the forest's highest point. From here, you enjoy uninterrupted views of the Coniston mountains. Dropping down to the busy visitor centre, there's a café awaiting you at the half-way point. After that, the walk climbs back into the forest, through more mixed woodland to the car park.

Grizedale Forest

Grizedale Forest, managed by the Forestry Commission, covers almost 25 square kilometres. Although mostly conifer plantations, there are a surprising variety of other woodland types too. The area is home to a wealth of wildlife, including red and roe deer, red kites, dormice, red squirrels, badgers, foxes and even the elusive pine marten. Tourism has become an important part of the forest economy in recent years with visitors drawn by sculpture trails, mountain biking routes, children's adventure playgrounds and a tree-top climbing course.

Panopticon sculpture

Red kite

The Walk

1. From the car park, head into the forest, bearing left at the first fork immediately after the barrier — signposted to 'Grizedale'. Ignore the track off to the right in a few metres.

2. At the next fork, bear right. Almost immediately, you will see two narrow trails on the left. The first is the **North Face mountain bike trail** — ignore this. Take the second one — which has a bridleway markerpost at the start of it.

As well as being popular with walkers, Grizedale Forest is a hub for mountain-bikers, so you need to be alert while on shared tracks. The North Face trail, however, is not open to walkers. It is a specially constructed, 16-kilometre route that winds its way through the trees and meadows, giving experienced bikers a chance to put their skills to the test. Like ski runs, mountain biking trails are colour graded. The North Face is a red (hard) trail.

Turn right along the next broad track and then, in a few metres, as this bends sharp left, take the steadily rising track on the right. Continue in the same direction after joining a wide forest track coming in from the right. You should be able to see a mast on the high ground of **Grizedale Moor** to your right in a short while.

3. At the next junction, turn left and, almost immediately, you reach a fork where you bear left again. In a few more metres, ignore the bridleway off to the left; keep to the higher, broader track.

4. Soon after passing and ignoring a turning to the right, the track bends left. As it does so, turn right along a narrow, stony path that climbs to the

Vantage point: *Carron Crag's 'trig' pillar is perched on a rocky outcrop*

open **summit of Carron Crag**. The 'trig' pillar sits on top of a small crag to the left of the path — most easily reached from its southern side.

With no other high ground for miles around, the views in all directions are far-reaching. The craggy Coniston fells, over to the north-west, look particularly enticing, but the Langdales and the Fairfield and Kentmere ranges are impressive too. To the south, the River Leven heads out into massive Morecambe Bay.

Continue on the path dropping away to the south of Carron Crag, following red and green marker posts and soon passing one of Grizedale Forest's many **sculptures**. The path down is steep, stony and wet in places.

5. Turn right on reaching a junction with a clear track. In a few more metres, you reach a three-way junction. Turn sharp left along the red, waymarked trail. At the next track, turn left. Almost immediately, turn right to descend the stony bridleway. Take the next path on the left — the red trail again. Having

Over the treetops: *The panoramic view of the Coniston fells from the top of Carron Crag*

descended some steps, bear left and then quickly turn right along a surfaced lane. You will soon see the **visitor centre** on your left, home to a **café**, **toilets**, **shop**, **children's adventure play area** and other facilities.

6. Turn left when you reach the road. Immediately after the house opposite the visitor centre — **Grizedale Hall Lodge** — head up the rough track to the right: signposted 'Esthwaite and Hawkshead'. This climbs along the edge of mixed woodland.

Don't forget to look up from the path occasionally for a chance of spotting the red kites that have recently been reintroduced to Grizedale Forest. These distinctive raptors were lost from the skies of north-west England — indeed from much of England and Scotland — in the second half of the nineteenth century. Today, their fortunes are looking up again; thanks to reintroduction programmes, which began in the 1980s, there are now up to 1,500 pairs nationally.

With their forked tails, long, angled wings and distinctive colouring, these large but graceful birds are unmistakeable in flight.

7. Turn left at the next track junction. The dense plantations that dominated the first part of the walk have now been replaced by tall, widely spaced trees that allow you snatched, tantalising glimpses of the mountains. Ignoring one turning on the right along the way, follow this broad track all the way to the road. Then turn right. The **Moor Top car park** where the walk started is 150 metres ahead on the left. ♦

Pine martens

In recent years, evidence has been found of pine martens living in Grizedale Forest. Due partly to hunting, poisoning and loss of habitat, this weasel-like mammal had become extinct throughout much of Britain by the early part of the 20th century. Small populations are thought to have survived in areas of northern England and Wales, with larger populations in the Scottish Highlands, where a recovery is now under way.

Staveley woods in late spring

Staveley's woods

A rhapsodic ramble along the River Kent and through a range of attractive woodland close to the village of Staveley

What to expect:
Quiet lanes, farm paths, woodland trails

Distance/time: 8.5km/ 5¼ miles. Allow 2¾-3¼ hours

Start: Mill Yard car park in Staveley

Grid ref: SD 471 983

Ordnance Survey Map: Explorer OL7 The English Lakes *South-eastern area, Windermere, Kendal & Silverdale*

After the walk: Wilf's Café, Mill Yard, Staveley, Kendal, Cumbria, LA8 9LR | www.wilfs-cafe.co.uk | 01539 822329 | info@wilfs-café.co.uk

Walk outline

The walk sets off from the thriving village of Staveley and uses quiet lanes and field paths to reach the first of the woods — Dorothy Farrer's Spring Wood. From here, more lanes drop down to the River Kent, where we follow a riverside trail through Beckmickle Ing. A complicated set of trails then leads past an attractive waterfall and up to some high ground to enter the last of the woods — Craggy Wood.

Staveley's woods

Each of the woodland visited on this walk has its own special qualities. Oak dominates Dorothy Farrer's Spring Wood, but hazel, elm, ash and alder are also present. In spring, the woodland floor is covered in bluebells and the air is alive with birdsong. The ancient riverside woodland of Beckmickle Ing has a wide mix of broadleaved trees and ground flora, including wild garlic (ransom), Solomon's seal and the pretty globeflower. The steep slopes of Craggy Wood, meanwhile, are home to some very grand beech trees, which create a thick, golden-brown carpet of leaves every autumn.

Craggy Wood sign

Globeflower

Blue and green: *Bluebells and fresh green spring leaves illuminate the woods around Staveley*

The Walk

1. From the car park's vehicle entrance, turn left and left again along **Staveley**'s main road. Take the path on the left after the **Duke William**. Cross the **River Kent** and turn right. Follow this path round to the left and go through a gate to access a lane. Turn right and immediately left — through a gate. Keeping close to the wall on the left at first, the path soon becomes clearer.

2. Turn right at the road. Having walked along the asphalt for 500 metres, cross the stile on the left. Head gently uphill beside the wall on your right.

3. At the top, you will see two tall gates into **Dorothy Farrer's Spring Wood**. Go through the one on the left. The trail follows the tumbling beck at first, but then swings right. Almost immediately, bear left through another tall gate — white arrows indicate the way. Soon after passing through a smaller, metal gate, keep left at a waymarked fork.

After reaching a wall at the woodland edge, the trail swings right and later begins descending. Watch carefully for the next waymarker; at this point, the trail becomes less distinct as it swings right — away from the wall. Dropping back on to the trail you followed earlier, turn left. Soon after the first tall gate, head off in a new direction by turning left. After a gate in a wall, keep straight ahead to reach a wide path. Turn left. Don't be tempted by a faint trail to the left after the next gate. The path heads around the back of a bungalow to emerge on its access lane.

4. Turn left to follow this downhill and around a sharp bend to the right. On reaching a minor road, turn right.

5. After about 200 metres on this road, go through the gap next to the Woodland Trust gate on the left. Follow the trail down through **Beckmickle Ing**, keeping close to the wall on your right at first. On reaching the **River Kent**, the trail swings left. Soon after a **bridge** over a tributary beck, turn left along a clearer path.

6. Turn right along the road and walk along the asphalt for 180 metres. Climb the steps and stile on the left — signposted to 'Side House'. There is no obvious path; the right-of-way heads north-north-west up the slope, crossing a stony track and then passing to the right of some woods. Go through a farm gate and head straight towards **Side House**.

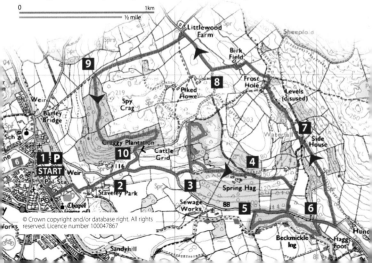

Brindled blue: *Bluebells colour the woods before the summer leaves shut out the light*

7. Walk to the left of the farmhouse and cross the beck. Immediately turn right to walk beside a wall on your left. Having climbed beside a **small waterfall**, go through a gate on the left and turn right along a grassy track.

On nearing the buildings at **Frost Hole**, go through the gate to cross the slope just below the property. After the next gate, turn right — over the beck. Once through the next gate, head uphill between two walls. Keep close to the one on the left and, as it swings left, you'll find yourself on a faint track. This goes through a gate and follows a small beck upstream. After the next gate, swing left, passing the cottage at **Birkfield**. Bear right up the farm lane.

8. Turn right at the T-junction. On reaching the next buildings, turn left through the yard and out through a metal gate — signposted 'Barley Bridge'. Keep close to the fence and wall on your left as you ascend. After a ladder stile, the wall is on your right. Beyond a second ladder stile, the wall disappears; simply head in the same direction, crossing two more ladder stiles.

9. After the second of these, turn left to enter the woods via a stile. After a while, the path goes through a gap in a wall to enter an area of beeches. The path keeps to the higher part of **Craggy Wood** at first, but later zig-zags downhill.

10. Turn right at the road and right again at the next junction. Go through the kissing-gate on your left to retrace your steps from the beginning of the walk. ♦

The versatile beech nut

Beech nuts, or 'mast', are a good source of energy and used to be eaten in times of famine. Although similar in taste to hazelnuts, they are small and fiddly to consume, so are today more likely to be used to fatten pigs or poultry. Roasted, they can also be used as a cheap coffee substitute. The oil from the crushed nuts is also suitable for cooking and to power oil-lamps.

Sunrise tints the morning mist over Grasmere

Grasmere's woods

A stroll through oak and bluebell woods, and a chance to enjoy one of the most captivating views in the Lake District

What to expect:
Mostly clear woodland and lakeside paths; short section on road

Distance/time: 5.5km/ 3¼ miles. Allow 1½-2 hours

Start: White Moss pay and display car park on the A591 between Grasmere and Rydal. There are two car parks at White Moss; the walk starts from the one on the southern side of the road

Grid ref: NY 350 065

Ordnance Survey Map: Explorer OL7 The English Lakes *South-eastern area, Windermere, Kendal & Silverdale*

After the walk: Glen Rothay Hotel & Badger Bar, Rydal, Ambleside, Cumbria LA22 9LR | www.theglenrothay.co.uk | 01539 434500

Walk outline

What could be more beguiling than the reflection of the woods and the fells in the calm waters of Grasmere? It's a spellbinding scene, and one that is seen from many angles on this walk. The route first approaches the lake via the River Rothay. After following the shore, it climbs easily into Redbank Wood and then out on to Loughrigg Terrace. Here, as you emerge from the trees, you are able to gaze down on the lake and the woods surrounding it.

Grasmere's woods

There is plenty of variety in the woodland at the southern end of Grasmere. The first part of the walk follows a path through the gorgeous, towering oaks of Penny Rock Wood. Later, Deer Bolts and Redbank woods provide a greater mix of conifers and broad-leaved species as well as the chance of spotting roe deer and red squirrels. Beyond Loughrigg Terrace, the walk drops back through an area that is, come May, awash with bluebells.

Fell gate

Roe deer at dawn

The Walk

1. The surfaced path starts from the **interpretation board** in the car park. Walk roughly west along this, through the woods. (There is a toilet block some metres up to the right early on.) You will see the **River Rothay** on your left, and then cross a small bridge over a tributary beck. Don't cross the larger bridge over the river, although you will cross it from the other side later in the walk. Instead, go through the gate and continue walking with the water on your left. After another two gates, you enter **Penny Rock Wood**. As you stroll through these oak woods, particularly gorgeous in the spring and autumn, keep left at any forks.

2. When the path drops back to river level, cross the gated bridge over the **River Rothay**.

This river links Grasmere with Rydal Water and later joins the River Brathay to enter Windermere at Ambleside.

Turn right to cross the beach at the southern end of **Grasmere** and then go through the gate on the far side of the shingle. In a few metres, head up the slope on the left to join a good track through the woods. Turn right along this. It never strays far from the lakeshore, and later emerges from the trees to continue beside the water.

The majestic fells that can be clearly seen to the north and east now include Seat Sandal, Great Rigg and Heron Pike.

About 800 metres after leaving the trees, the permissive path performs a sharp bend to the left, away from the lakeshore.

3. When you reach the road, turn right. Walk along the asphalt for 130 metres and then turn left along a narrow, surfaced lane — just as you

Green mirror: *The footbridge below Loughrigg Terrace at Grasmere's eastern end*

draw level with a cottage on your right with a postbox in its wall. The lane goes over to cobbles as it climbs more steeply between moss-covered, drystone walls.

4. About 500 metres after leaving the road, you will see a bench on the right. Turn left here, through a gate — signposted 'Loughrigg Terrace'. Contouring the hillside, this good path provides a higher view of the lake, glimpsed occasionally through the trees on your left.

You might be lucky enough to spot red squirrels in these woods, although they are slowly being replaced by their North American grey cousins in some parts of the Lake District. You probably have a greater chance, particularly at dawn or dusk, of seeing roe deer. These are distinguished from red deer by their fluffy white bottoms and the white patches around their mouths.

The path leaves the woods via another gate and cuts across a bracken-covered slope. There are a couple of benches on this section of path if you need to rest,

Golden mirror: *Grasmere's tranquil waters reflect the reds and yellows of autumn*

but there are some far superior benches coming up soon if you can wait.

5. At the road, turn right and walk along the asphalt for just 100 metres. Then turn left along a path heading downhill.

6. You later go through an old metal kissing-gate to access the lower slopes of **Loughrigg Fell**. Ignoring the path heading steeply uphill on your right, walk along **Loughrigg Terrace**, high above Grasmere. There are several well placed benches here, enabling you to enjoy the views.

This excellent path sits at the base of Loughrigg Fell's bracken-covered northern slopes. The view of the lake from here is mesmerising, and its surrounding woods look particularly resplendent during the autumn. The eye is also drawn to the smooth sweep of Dunmail Raise, the pass on the A591. To its west, the steep slopes rise to Steel Fell; to the east is Seat Sandal. In the distance, framed in the gap, is Lonscale Fell, an outlier of Skiddaw.

Ignore one trail to the right and continue along the terrace path until you reach a path junction close to a wall. Turn right here and walk downhill beside the wall for about 70 metres.

7. When you reach another path on your right, go through the gate in the wall on the left. This drops down through the woods, eventually reaching the banks of the **River Rothay**. Cross the **footbridge** that you ignored at the start of the walk and then turn right along the clear path. Retracing your steps from earlier, keep right at a fork to return to the car park where the walk started. ◆

Bluebells

It is thought the UK is home to up to half of the world's bluebell population. The popular species usually dwells in woods, flowering in spring before the canopy thickens and prevents ample sunlight from reaching the ground. In western Britain, it can also be found in more open areas. As well as among the trees above the River Rothay, look out for it on the lower slopes of Loughrigg Fell before you re-enter the woods.

Tall pines, like cathedral columns, in Haverthwaite's woods

Haverthwaite Heights

A rolling ramble through varied woodland on the southern edge of the Lake District

What to expect:
Woodland paths; potentially confusing in Massicks Wood

Distance/time: 3.5km/ 2¼ miles. Allow 1½-2 hours

Start: Small layby on minor road between River Leven and the Lakeside and Haverthwaite Railway, Backbarrow. Travelling south along the A590, turn right 2km south of Newby Bridge. Layby on the left, about 100 metres after the road crosses the River Leven.

Grid ref: SD 355 848

Ordnance Survey Map: Explorer OL6 The English Lakes *South-western area, Coniston, Ulverston and Barrow-in-Furness*

After the walk: The Whitewater Hotel, Newby Bridge, Cumbria, England LA12 8PX | www.whitewater-hotel.co.uk | 01539 531133

Walk outline

This surprisingly tough little roller-coaster of a route uses permissive paths and trails to explore a beautiful area of mixed woodland among the rolling hills close to the southern end of Windermere. It reaches a high point of 156 metres in Massicks Wood. Although the top is not completely clear of trees, there are some good views of the Levens Estuary leading out into Morecambe Bay.

Haverthwaite Heights

Covering 75 hectares and owned by the Lake District National Park Authority, Haverthwaite Heights is at least 400 years old. As you wander its trails, you'll encounter mature yews, oak, birch, a few gnarled old Scots pines and, at the northern limit of their UK distribution, small-leaved lime trees. You will also see areas of larch as well as conifer plantations, but these have largely been replaced by native broadleaved trees. Foxgloves, bluebells and celandines thrive on the woodland floor and, on the higher ground of Massicks Wood, dense thickets of bilberry can be found.

Starting out

Lesser celandines

The Walk

1. From the layby, cross the road and walk under the railway. At the top of the first, short rise, turn right. The path, clearly marked by white-topped posts, winds its way steadily uphill. Bear left along a broader, level path and then, within a few metres, turn right at a fingerpost.

2. On reaching the highest ground in **Massicks Wood**, you will see a solitary Scots pine to the left of the trail. Keep straight on, ignoring the faint trail to the left. About 15 metres after crossing a tumbledown wall, bear right at an easy-to-miss fork. This quickly mounts a tiny, bracken and heather-covered ridge. Ignore the faint trail to the right here. The path soon starts heading downhill to the right — towards a waymarker post. Beyond this, it heads generally south-west.

3. On reaching a clearer path marked by a fingerpost, turn right.

4. Turn left at **Lane Ends** along a quiet lane. (There is alternative parking here if the layby near Backbarrow is full.) Go through the gate at the end of the lane and head up the grassy track. Ignore a track heading left. When the fence on your right ends, you will see another track going left, a trail to the right beside an old wall and a track straight ahead. Take this middle track, following it for about 80 metres. Then, on reaching a waymarker post, turn right along a narrow trail.

Don't be tempted by a muddy trail to the right after 150 metres; simply keep to the clearest path. It climbs gently,

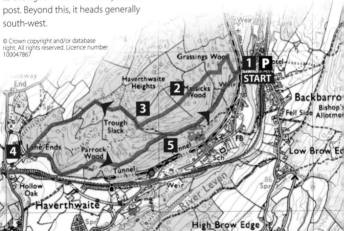

Dappled shade: *Sunlight and shadow enliven the depths of Massicks Wood*

often with an old, moss-covered wall on the right. After the first climb, you reach an area of yew trees; the understorey here is dominated by holly.

5. Turn right on reaching a clearer path. In a few more metres, ignore the trail to the right; simply keep straight on. About 120 metres beyond this junction, bear left at a fork. Another 200 metres will bring you to a less obvious fork in an area of tall, widely spaced conifers. Bear right, heading downhill on a carpet of pine needles, eventually passing back under the **railway** to return to where the walk started. ♦

Fuelling the furnaces

The woodland on Haverthwaite Heights was once coppiced for charcoal. The timber was slowly heated, with a carefully regulated supply of air, to produce a coal-like substance that was then used in industry. The charcoal would probably have been used as fuel in the iron furnaces at Backbarrow and in the gunpowder mill at Low Wood, both of which thrived in the eighteenth and nineteenth centuries.

Muncaster Castle sits on raised ground amid dense woods

Muncaster Estate

Sea views, fells, colourful Himalayan shrubs, bluebell woods and more on a walk through a Lake District estate

What to expect:
Estuarine path, woodland tracks and faint trails; some road walking

Distance/time: 9.5km/ 6 miles. Allow 2¾-3¼ hours

Start: Main Lake District National Park car park in Ravenglass

Grid ref: SD 085 964

Ordnance Survey Map: Explorer OL 6 The English Lakes *South-western area. Coniston, Ulverston & Barrow-in-Furness*

After the walk: The Ratty Arms, Ravenglass, Cumbria, CA18 1SN
www.rattyarms.co.uk | 01229 717676 | rattyarms@aol.com

Walk outline

You'll need to consult tide timetables before setting off on this walk from the pretty seaside village of Ravenglass. It first ventures out on to the estuary of the River Esk before heading upstream along a superb woodland track with views of the mountains at the head of Eskdale. After some road walking, the route enters the woods of the Muncaster Estate, awash with colour in the spring. The final part of the walk provides excellent views of the coast and, on a clear day, across to the Isle of Man.

Roman bath house

Muncaster Estate

The route passes through two distinct areas of woodland on the Muncaster Estate: the mixed woods beside the River Esk and the more formal gardens surrounding the castle itself. The latter includes one of Europe's largest collections of rhododendron. Native to the foothills of the Himalayas, these exotic shrubs burst into vibrant colour every May, as do the bluebells that carpet the woodland floor. Camellias, magnolias, azaleas, bamboo and daffodils are also present.

Long-eared owl

The Walk

1. Leave the car park via its vehicle entrance and turn left along the dead-end road. Take the next lane on the right. Turn left at the road and then head down the **slipway**. Bear left along the shingle, soon swinging right as you follow the **River Esk**.

About 1 kilometre beyond the slipway, the fairly solid ground gives way to a gloopy mud-bank. This can be avoided by using a narrow path through the grass, keeping close to the fence at first. The river soon swings east. A grassy path leads through a gate and under the **railway**.

2. Just before you draw level with buildings on the opposite bank, go through a gate on your left. The narrow path quickly reaches a wider track near a **Cumbria Coastal Way** signpost. Turn right here. This shady track makes for lovely walking. As you progress, various mountains appear in the distance, including Scafell, Bow Fell and Crinkle Crags.

3. About 1.2 kilometres after joining the track, it climbs slightly and swings left. As it does so, bear right along a narrow, waymarked trail through the trees. After dropping down some steps, turn left along a faint track. About 50 metres along this, watch for a waymarker showing the trail going off to the right. This **fords a tiny beck** and then crosses another via a **footbridge**.

Turn left to walk with a fence on your right and then go through a kissing-gate. Bear half-left, passing beneath **Muncaster Castle**, to reach a wooden post and then walk up towards a

Blue is the colour: *Swathes of wild bluebells carpet the woodland floor in early summer*

fingerpost. On reaching it, turn right along the track.

4. Turn left along the busy A595. Be careful because traffic moves fast along this road. Having walked for about 900 metres on the asphalt, go through a wooden gate in the wall on the left. You are now entering the grounds of Muncaster Castle, and you must keep to the rights-of-way: the subsidiary trails and tracks should only be accessed by ticket-holders.

5. Turn right along the track and right again at the next junction. Continue for a few more metres and then take the path on the right — into the **churchyard**. Exit via the **lych gate** and turn left along Muncaster Castle's access road. On reaching a **play area**, keep straight ahead, crossing a grassy area to the left of a **pond**. Turn left along the track and bear right when it splits — signposted 'Ravenglass via Newtown'.

In spring, this section of the woods is awash with colour. Early in the season, the camellias, magnolias and daffodils are

Riverside path: *The woodland track follows the broad tidal River Esk upstream*

in bloom; later, in May, it is the turn of the rhododendrons and azaleas. Higher up in **Dovecote Wood**, *the springtime colour is provided by a more traditional plant: the bluebell.*

Keep straight on until the track splits next to a particularly impressive *Sino-Grande rhododendron*. Bear right here. Keep right again, leaving the woods via a gate.

6. With jaw-dropping views out to sea, which include the Isle of Man, head south-west across this open, pathless area. Enter the next area of woodland via a stile to the right of a particularly tightly packed group of trees. Head down the trail, beside a railing at first and then through a dark area of conifers. About 200 metres into the trees, watch for a fingerpost on your right. Swing left here to leave the woods via a gate.

7. Turn right along the track, ignoring a turning to Muncaster on the right in a short while. At the next junction, turn right — there is a path to the right of the asphalt for pedestrians. Pick up the footpath again after **Walls Castle**.

In Roman times, Ravenglass was an important naval base and supply depot.

Little remains today of the Roman fort of Glannoventa, *except for 'Walls Castle', which was the bath house. With 3.5 metre-high walls, this is the tallest Roman structure in northern England.*

When the path ends, continue along the lane in the same direction. Just before the main road, turn left beside some cottages. After crossing the railway, turn right to re-enter the car park. ♦

Himalayan invader

Although rhododendron is sometimes lovely to look at, this non-native plant has become a big problem in many areas. First introduced to Britain at the end of the eighteenth century, it spread quickly, forming an understorey that allows little light through and prevents native plants and shrubs from growing. Some landowners, such as the National Trust, put a lot of effort into eradicating it from their estates.

The River Liza tumbles through the remote Ennerdale valley

Ennerdale

A wild riverside walk through the forests of one of the Lake District's most remote valleys, towered over by craggy peaks

What to expect:
Forest track; riverside and woodland paths

Distance/time: 13km/8 miles. Allow 3¼-3¾ hours

Start: Bowness Knott car park on the northern side of Ennerdale Water

Grid ref: NY 109 153

Ordnance Survey Map: Explorer OL 4 The English Lakes *North-western area. Keswick, Cockermouth & Wigton*

After the walk: Fox and Hounds, Ennerdale Bridge, Cumbria, CA23 3AR | www.foxandhoundsinn.org | 01946 861 373
info@foxandhoundsinn.org

Walk outline

After leaving the track that runs beside Ennerdale Water, the route heads upstream along the partially wooded south bank of the River Liza. The return is via a broad track with an opportunity to take a short detour up into the forest proper.

Ennerdale

With few dwellings and no roads, Ennerdale is probably the loneliest of the major Lake District dales. And it's fast becoming the wildest too... The closely packed, regimented lines of sitka spruces that once dominated the valley are slowly disappearing. This is thanks to Ennerdale's primary landowners — the National Trust, the Forestry Commission and United Utilities — who, in 2003, formed a partnership called Wild Ennerdale, which aims to 'allow the evolution of Ennerdale as a wild valley for the benefit of people, relying more on natural processes to shape its landscape and ecology'.

Remote cottage

Ten years into the project and the appearance of this valley is already changing — broadleaf trees are returning and the River Liza is being allowed to chart its own course.

Otter

The Walk

1. Turn left out of the car park. With **Ennerdale Water** on your right and mixed woodland on the left, follow this wide track up into the valley for 2.5 kilometres.

2. Just after passing the far, eastern end of the lake, turn right to cross the **Char Dub bridge**. Go through the gate at the end of the track and turn left. Soon after crossing the **bridge over Woundell Beck**, the wide track approaches a large gate. Leave it here by bearing left to go through a kissing-gate just below the track.

3. The trail, faint in places, keeps close to the tall conifers on your right and then follows the top of the riverbank.

The Wild Ennerdale philosophy is to allow nature a greater say in the valley's future. Nowhere is this lack of human interference more evident than in the wide, meandering River Liza. Probably one of the most natural rivers in England, it is not constrained in any way. In fact, when the river changed course in a storm a few years ago and overwhelmed a public right of way, a decision was made not to divert the new channel but to divert the path instead.

The Liza's substantial shingle beds are home to a rare type of stiletto fly. The larvae live just beneath the surface and can detect the vibrations of prey above. Stealthily, they position themselves underneath the prey and pierce it with stiletto-like mouthparts, injecting poison that instantly paralyses. They then drag their prey under the shingle.

Blue arch: *Looking back down Ennerdale Water towards Anglers' Crag*

Soon after crossing a small wooden bridge, bear left along a grassy track that skirts the northern edge of **Moss Dub**. At the eastern end of the tiny lake, turn left along a narrow, easy-to-miss trail to regain the riverside path.

You now pass through an area of forest that came down in the big storm of January 2005. This has been partially cleared to allow more open woodland to develop, but fallen trees are also being allowed to decay. These provide a habitat for insects, beetles, fungi and lichens.

There is an elongated pile of stones in the next clearing. This is the remains of an Iron Age settlement. Just after the settlement, you cross two small bridges in quick succession. You then get your first good view of **Pillar** and the mountains to the south of **Ennerdale**.

All along this section of the river, broadleaf trees and heather are returning — filling the gaps left by felled conifers. Oak, birch, rowan and willow are returning. Spruce is

River wild?: *Unchecked by man, the River Liza is creating its own changing course*

allowed to regrow for the sake of diversity, but it is removed if it starts dominating — as has happened further up the valley.

As you continue upstream, the **River Liza** gets ever wilder as it carves a route through a narrow, rocky channel.

4. On reaching a wide forest track, turn left and cross the river via the bridge. Ignoring a track up to the right, you now swing left to start your downstream journey. Just beyond **Ennerdale Youth Hostel** at Gillerthwaite, keep right at a fork. After passing the **Char Dub bridge**

that you crossed earlier in the walk, it's simply a case of retracing your steps along the track to the car park.

Alternatively, a tiny detour along part of the **Smithy Beck trail** will take you further into the forest for little extra effort: it's only a few hundred metres longer than following the main track and an extra 30 metres or so of climbing.

5. For the detour, turn right on a faint path about 1 kilometre beyond the **Char Dub bridge** — immediately after crossing **Smithy Beck**. It has a red waymarker post, although this is set back from the track. At a junction close to a bridge by a small waterfall, turn left.

Keep your eyes peeled for wildlife among the trees: otters have recolonised the valley, both red and roe deer frequent the area, and there have even been unconfirmed sightings of the elusive pine marten.

The path crosses **Dry Beck** via a small bridge, before dropping back down to the lakeside track, along which you turn right to return to the car park. ♦

Beefy beasts

Semi-wild Galloway cattle were introduced to the valley in 2006 when ecologists advised the Wild Ennerdale team that the disturbance caused by large herbivores was necessary to open the way for different plant species. Like everything else in the valley, they are mostly left to their own devices. Calves are born unaided — the mother going off to a secluded place to give birth, returning to the herd a few days later.

Looking over the trees towards Bassenthwaite Lake

Dodd Wood

An atmospheric walk through the forests at the base of Skiddaw — with views of Bassenthwaite Lake

What to expect:
Good forest paths and tracks

Distance/time: 5km/ 3 miles. Allow 1¾-2¼ hours

Start: Forestry Commission's Dodd Wood pay and display car park near Bassenthwaite

Grid ref: NY 235 281

Ordnance Survey Map: Explorer OL 4 The English Lakes *Northwestern area. Keswick, Cockermouth & Wigton*

After the walk: Old Sawmill Tearoom (in the car park), Dodd Wood, Mirehouse, Keswick, Cumbria, CA12 5TW | www.theoldsawmill. co.uk | 01768 774317 | whinlatter@forestry.gsi.gov.uk

Walk outline

This short, undulating walk passes through a variety of woodland types within the narrow, northern arm of Dodd Wood. Excellent paths make for easy walking, with plenty of opportunity to watch for wildlife and to enjoy glimpses of Bassenthwaite Lake and the lower slopes of Skiddaw.

Dodd Wood

Forestry Commission woodland isn't all dark, regimented conifers. Although there are still some sections of Dodd Wood that consist of such dense plantations, the forest contains a surprisingly wide range of tree types. One minute you can be walking under a thick canopy with little sign of the sky above and a carpet of pine needles underfoot; the next you're striding out along a broad path lined by slender birches.

The woods are home to red squirrels, badgers and foxes, but the most famous residents are the ospreys that nest here every summer. The walk includes a short detour to the osprey viewing platform, which also provides a superb outlook over the lake.

Woodland path

Forest fox

The Walk

1. Cross the bridge behind the **tearoom** and turn left at the top of the first short slope. Turn left along a surfaced track. Cross the coach parking area to pick up the continuation of the path through the trees. The mostly level route runs parallel with the main road through mixed woodland — at one point crossing straight over another track close to some bee hives.

2. Soon after crossing a **footbridge**, the track begins climbing into thicker forest. Leave it here by turning left along a narrower path. This then crosses a parking area and continues beyond a barrier.

3. As you near the **Ravenstone Hotel**, you will see a narrow path heading uphill to the right. Take this. With views over **Bassenthwaite Lake**, climb to a crossing of paths where you go straight over, continuing uphill into thicker, conifer forest. In a particularly dark part of the woods, you are joined by a track coming in from the left at a yellow path-marker. You soon cross a footbridge over **Sandbeds Gill**, after which the trees thin out.

4. Just after passing a yellow path-marker on your right and an outcrop of rock on your left, bear left at a junction of paths. From the junction at the top of the first rise, you get a clear view ahead

of the top of Dodd. Keep left at the next fork.

5. Eventually, you drop on to a surfaced track. Turn left along this, taking just a few strides uphill before you turn right to head downhill to a **bridge across Skill Beck**. The path then swings back on itself to meet a wider track coming

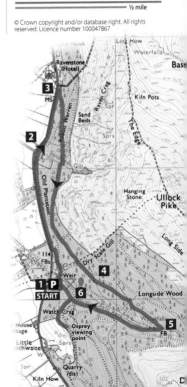

Lonesome pines: *A young walker pauses among the mature pines of Dodd Wood*

down from the left. Bearing right here, you pass a number of red path-markers as you walk downhill. Dropping back into the trees, bear right at the next junction of tracks and then right again a few metres later as the descent steepens. You are now following green and red path-markers.

6. At a faint crossing of paths, the main route turns right to descend back to the **car park**. Alternatively, turn left and then keep straight on at a junction for a short detour to the **osprey viewing point**. ♦

Bassenthwaite ospreys
The Forestry Commission and National Park spent years trying to encourage ospreys back to Cumbria after they were persecuted to extinction in Britain. They built tree-top platforms for the birds, and, in 2001, a passing pair took a fancy to one of these 'nests' near Bassenthwaite Lake. The fish-eating birds of prey now arrive in the county every April and return to Africa in September, having reared a small family.

The curious Bowder Stone painted by autumn sunlight

Ashness Woods

A walk through craggy Borrowdale woodland and on to a low, heathery summit with grand mountain and lake views

Distance/time: 4km/ 2¼ miles. Allow 2-2½ hours

Start: National Trust's Bowder Stone car park in Borrowdale

Grid ref: NY 253 168

Ordnance Survey Map: Explorer OL 4 The English Lakes *North-western area. Keswick, Cockermouth & Wigton*

After the walk: Flock-In Tearooms, Yew Tree Farm, Rosthwaite, Borrowdale, Cumbria, CA12 5XB | www.borrowdaleyewtreefarm.co.uk | 01768 777675 | relphs@btinternet.com

Walk outline

This route on to King's How (392 metres) involves a steep ascent and descent, but there are plenty of rewards to be had. Borrowdale's woods are among the finest in the whole of the Lake District and, once you've reached the heathery summit, you gain a bird's-eye view over this magnificent, tree-filled valley as well as Derwentwater and Skiddaw. The final part of the walk is on a track providing access to the impressive Bowder Stone.

Ashness Woods

The Ashness Woods stretch from Ashness Bridge almost all the way to Rosthwaite. In places, as around King's How, the trees cling to steep, crag-bound fellsides. Here, the woodland is dominated by birch and oak, making for breathtaking walking on a sunny, autumnal day. A few ancient yews and occasional Scots pines provide a splash of green during the colourless winter months. Watch for red deer in the woods and, early in the year, listen for the Borrowdale cuckoo heralding the arrival of spring.

Edward VII memorial

Cuckoo

The Walk

1. From the top parking area (immediately above the picnic benches), head to the far side of the car park (opposite to where you entered) and you will see a small wooden gate in a fence below. Go through this and walk along the faint trail through the trees. This soon passes a few metres to the left of a **large boulder** and then goes through a small, **disused quarry.** Climbing gently through an open area, ignore any trails off to the left. The path swings right through an area of bracken and light birch wood.

2. On attaining a **small ridge**, you reach a faint crossing of paths: there's a boulder off to the right here. Go straight over, dropping through a gate in a wall. As the path swings right in a short while, ignore a trail to the left. Drop into a small dip and then begin climbing more steeply beneath **Greatend Crag**. On reaching a right-hand bend in the path, don't be tempted by a faint trail to the left. The next section of steep path is partially pitched, making the ascent a little easier than it might otherwise be. Eventually, the gradient eases and you cross an almost flat area. Ignore a stile in a fence down to the left. Immediately after this, the path swings right and begins climbing again.

3. At the top of the next short climb, the path skirts the edge of a **boggy area**.

Immediately after passing beneath a **solitary yew**, it begins climbing again — quite steeply in places. Small birch trees are scattered about as the woods begin to thin out; you might also spot holly growing from some of the rocky knolls. At an indistinct fork above a tumbledown wall, don't be tempted by the trail heading down to the right; instead, bear left to climb steeply. You leave the trees behind now as you make your way up on to the heather-clad hill. Ignore a narrow, cairned trail to the left

0 _____ 1km
  _____
  ½ mile

© Crown copyright and/or database right. All rights reserved. Licence number 100047867

Lakeland roots: *A beech tree's smooth, muscled roots cling to a riverside slope*

and you will soon pass a **memorial to King Edward VII** set into the rock on your left.

King's How, which is owned by the National Trust, was named as a memorial to Kind Edward VII in 1910. The memorial plaque states that the fell was dedicated by his sister Louise 'as a sanctuary of rest and peace'.

4. There are impressive views to be had from the unmarked **summit of King's How**. *Take some time to look around: Skiddaw and Derwentwater to the north, the Helvellyn range to the east and Borrowdale to the south. The latter is enclosed by a striking array of mountains that includes Glaramara, Base Brown and Dale Head.*

From the summit, the path continues south-south-east, down one rocky section and then swinging sharp left after a second one. The route is grassier now as it continues downhill with views of Borrowdale ahead. Keep right at a fork (south-south-west, later veering south-south-east).

Golden days: *Autumnal tints reflected in Borrowdale's tranquil River Derwent*

5. On nearing a wall, bear right at a fork — ignoring the gap in the wall and soon descending with the wall on your left. You can see across to Castle Crag now, pockmarked by several quarry pits, clearly visible even at this distance. The descent becomes a lot steeper as you re-enter the woods. The path later crosses a tumbledown section of wall, after which you'll pass a particularly **fine old yew** to the right of the path. Continue descending, ignoring any lesser trails. Nearing the road, you'll see another large yew. The path swings right here, soon dropping to the road.

6. Turn right and walk along the **B5289** for about 150 metres. Then go through a gate on the right — signposted to the 'Bowder Stone'. This provides access to a rough track, climbing gently.

*The **400-million-year-old Bowder Stone** has been a magnet for tourists since Victorian times. More than 30 feet high, about 90 feet in circumference and balanced apparently precariously on one edge, it was probably left here by a passing glacier. It has a secure wooden ladder up the side of it, should you wish to reach the top. The woods here are mostly oak, although there are occasional Scots pines scattered about.*

The track goes through a gate and passes some old quarry workings that are now used for abseiling. On dropping to the road again, climb the slate steps on your right — just behind the bus stop. Turn right along the car park's access lane to return to where the walk started. ♦

Long live the yew
Yew trees, one of Britain's three native conifers, have been found to live for thousands of years, making them our longest living plant. Not only that, but the timber's longevity continues long after the tree has been felled: one of the world's oldest wooden artefacts is a spear head made from yew. It was found in Essex in 1911, and is believed to be at least 250,000 years old.

Looking down on Ullswater from Place Fell

Silver Crag

An excellent low-level walk close to the shores of Ullswater, including a visit to a juniper-topped crag

What to expect:
Good low-level tracks and paths, less well-defined on detours

Distance/time: 6.5km/ 4 miles. Allow 2-2¼ hours

Start: George Starkey Hut in Patterdale

Grid ref: NY 394 160

Ordnance Survey Map: Explorer OL 5 The English Lakes North-eastern area. *Penrith, Patterdale & Caldbeck*

After the walk: The White Lion Inn, Patterdale, Cumbria, CA11 0NW | www.thewhitelioninnpatterdale.co.uk | 01768 482214 info@thewhitelioninnpatterdale.co.uk

Walk outline

After heading north from Patterdale to visit Silver Point, a craggy promontory sticking out into Ullswater, the walk climbs slightly to return via a superb path running parallel with the outward route but slightly higher up the slopes of Place Fell. This small gain in altitude makes all the difference, turning good views into breathtaking panoramas. A short detour to the top of tiny Silver Crag (271 metres) provides more of those wonderful views.

Silver Crag

Don't expect to be walking among towering trees on this more unusual woodland walk: Silver Crag and the slopes of Birk Fell represent one of the last big strongholds of the juniper tree, which, even at its tallest, is no more than four metres in height. The Lake District used to be covered in huge forests of the stuff, but much of it has gone now. Its decline has been particularly marked over the last 50 years with many old bushes not being naturally replaced owing to grazing pressures and shading from other plants.

Gnarled juniper roots

Badger

The Walk

1. Walk along the track on the northern side of the **George Starkey Hut** in Patterdale. It goes through the yard at **Side Farm**, passing to the left of the farmhouse. (On summer weekends, one of the out-buildings here serves ice-creams and drinks.)

2. Turn left along the wide track at the back of the buildings. This quickly goes through a large gate, passing between stands of oak and ash. Do not be tempted by any of the other gates to the left of the track as you make your way out to **Silver Point**.

The gently undulating track is straightforward, easily fording a few small becks as it heads north. Eventually, the wall swings away and you get a great, uninterrupted view across the lake towards **Glenridding**. Scots pine soon dominate the woodland on the left. The path now drops slightly as it skirts the lakeside.

Up to the right are the slopes of Silver Crag, thickly cloaked in juniper bushes — and the occasional holly. If you get a chance, squeeze one of the juniper berries and then sniff it. There's no mistaking which spirit this is used to flavour. Did anyone think to bring the tonic? In the 17th century, the herbalist Nicholas Culpepper recommended the berries as a treatment for asthma and sciatica. He also claimed they could speed childbirth.

Attempts are now being made in some parts of Cumbria to replant areas with young juniper bushes. In Longsleddale a few years ago, climbers were brought in to plant the conifers on inaccessible crags where they would be safe from sheep. The

Messing about on the water: *A tiny boat in Ullswater's Silver Bay*

berries provide an important source of food for birds and animals such as field mice, squirrels and badgers.

Before long, you reach a high point as the path swings slightly right — and you can see across to **Gowbarrow**.

3. For a brief detour on to **Silver Point** itself, leave the main path in a short while by turning left along a faint, grassy path. Steep crags plummet suddenly into the water below, while a grassy shore and shingle beach below provide a perfect spot for a picnic. Having enjoyed the views from the headland, return to the main path and continue in the same direction as before.

In a short while, you will see a pitched path heading uphill on the right. Take this, climbing at a moderate angle to a secret valley between **Silver Crag** on your right and **Birk Fell** on your left. In summer, this is a sylvan gap in the mountains, but, come winter, bitingly cold winds cut through here, making it feel quite wild.

Golden evening: *Ullswater from Place Fell in low, evening light*

---

4. For a short detour to the **top of Silver Crag**, watch for a faint trail on the right as you approach the southern end of this valley. Take this and, when it splits, bear right again to climb quickly to the summit. A narrow path fights its way through the forest of head-height juniper that covers the top, but it's worth the effort; there are great views across to the Helvellyn range and towards Kirkstone Pass.

Retrace your steps back down to the little valley and then turn right. A gorgeous grassy path now stretches out in the front of you. Follow it as it traverses the fellside, about 50 metres above the track that you followed on the way out. The little bit of extra height provides a surprisingly different perspective on your surroundings.

Ignore any paths to the right that will take you back down to the main track. You pass a green, **Victorian bench**, beyond which the path drops slightly, passing some dramatic **old quarry** workings on the way. Approaching piles of slate at the next set of workings, the path forks. Take either branch, although the one to the left is slightly easier.

5. The path forks again above some cottages. Turn right here, dropping to cross a tiny bridge. Go through the large gate to gain access to the top of a lane. Turn right along the rough farm track.

When you reach **Side Farm**, turn left between the farm buildings and retrace your steps to the **George Starkey Hut** where the walk started. ♦

Cumbria's conifers

There are only three conifers native to Britain and two of them are seen on this walk: juniper and Scot's pine. Both are typical in that they have needle-like leaves and bear their fruit in cones. The third, yew, seen on walk No. 9, is an exception because its fruit is contained in a red 'berry'. All three are evergreens, but not all conifers are evergreen: larch, for example, sheds its leaves every autumn. The photo here shows juniper berries.

Useful Information

Cumbria Tourism

Cumbria Tourism's official website covers everything from accommodation and events to attractions and adventure. **www.golakes.co.uk**

Lake District National Park

The Lake District National Park website also has information on things to see and do, plus maps, webcams and news. **www.lakedistrict.gov.uk**

Tourist Information Centres

The main TICs provide free information on everything from accommodation and travel to what's on and walking advice.

Ambleside	01539 432 582	tic@thehubofambleside.com
Bowness	01539 442 895	bownesstic@lake-district.gov.uk
Coniston	01539 441 533	mail@conistontic.org
Keswick	01768 772 645	keswicktic@lake-district.gov.uk
Penrith	01768 867 466	pen.tic@eden.gov.uk
Ullswater	01768 482 414	ullswatertic@lake-district.gov.uk
Windermere	01539 446 499	windermeretic@southlakeland.gov.uk

Forestry Commission

Two Forestry Commission teams manage Cumbria's forests and woodlands, as well as Visitor Centres, Education and Recreation services and the Lake District Osprey Project.

North Cumbria team (Whinlatter) | 01768 778469 | adrian.jones@forestry.gsi.gov.uk
South Cumbria team (Grizedale) | 01229 860373 | david.lowe@forestry.gov.uk

National Trust

The National Trust cares for around a quarter of the land within the Lake District National Park, including many important landscapes, lakes and woods.

National Trust, The Hollens, Grasmere, Cumbria, LA22 9QZ | 01539 435353 |
nw.customerenquiries@nationaltrust.org.uk

Both the **Woodland Trust** and **Cumbria Wildlife Trust** also own interesting woods in the Lake District, many of which are accessible to the public.

Weather

Five day forecast for the Lake District: 0844 846 2444
www.lakedistrict.gov.uk/weatherline